Published by Creative Education
123 South Broad Street, Mankato, Minnesota 56001
Creative Education is an imprint of The Creative Company

Designed by Stephanie Blumenthal
Production Design by Melinda Belter

Photographs by Auscape, Healesville Sancutuary, C.A. Henley, C. Allan Morgan,
James P. Rowan, Tom Stack and Associates, Dave Watts

Library of Congress Cataloging-in-Publication Data

Gaines, Ann Graham.
Platypus / by Ann Graham Gaines
p. cm. — (Let's Investigate)
Includes bibliographical references
Includes glossary and index
Summary: Describes the physical characteristics and behavior of platypuses, one
of three species of monotremes, or egg laying mammals.
ISBN 0-88682-612-8
1. Platypus—Juvenile literature. [1. Platypus.] I. title. II. Series. III. Series:
Let's Investigate (Mankato, Minn.)
QL737.M72G35   1999
599.2'9—dc21   98-20896

First edition

2 4 6 8 9 7 5 3 1

PLATYPUS

ANN GRAHAM GAINES

Creative C Education

PLATYPUS

POLAR

Researchers believe that Antarctica was once tropical and home to platypuses.

PLATYPUS

HEALTH

Platypus milk contains 60 times more iron than cow milk.

Above, riverbanks are home to the platypus Right, platypuses swim in warm water

Animals come in all shapes and sizes, but think of a unique animal the length of a small cat, with stout legs, thick fur, and a paddle tail like a beaver's. Add a flat bill like a duck's and webbed feet with claws. This animal may sound like an imaginary creature, but it's not—it's the duck-billed platypus!

These fantastic little animals have astounded scientists for more than 200 years.

PLATYPUS
A R T

Thousands of years ago, ancient Aborigines made rock paintings and carvings of platypuses.

PLATYPUS
P E S T S

Australia had no rabbits until Europeans brought them. They soon became pests, eating the grasses meant for sheep and cattle, and forcing platypuses to compete for riverbanks.

Platypuses in captivity

PLATYPUS DISCOVERY

European scientists first saw a platypus skin in 1798. They could not believe their eyes, and so they decided that it must be a **hoax.** In 1802 Everard Home, a famous scientist who examined another platypus skin, said the animal was real, though few people believed him.

Many years later, when it was finally agreed that the platypus was a true product of nature, the next step was to decide whether or not it should be considered a **mammal.**

The 1884 discovery that platypuses lay eggs only increased confusion about the animal. Scientists from around the world were eager to study the platypus.

In 1922, after a 49-day boat trip from Australia, the first platypus to be held in captivity arrived at the Bronx Zoo in New York, but it died just 47 days later. Three more arrived in 1947; one lived only a year, but the other two lived for ten years. Over the decades that followed, the platypus has been the subject of continued research.

MYTH

The platypus body resembles that of the beaver.

TRUTH

The platypus is actually much smaller and has fur on its tail.

Below, echidna

PLATYPUS

NICKNAMES

European settlers of Australia called the platypus a water mole; the Aborigines call the platypus a jimmialong.

PLATYPUS

MEAL

On a typical day, a large male platypus can eat 20 or 30 crayfish, 200 mealworms, and two small frogs.

Australian wildlife includes the ring-tail possum (top) and koalas (bottom) Opposite, platypus foraging for food

Today zoologists recognize the platypus as a mammal, but a very peculiar one. More than 4,000 species of mammals live on Earth. Almost all of them give birth to live young. Platypuses and their closest relatives, the **echidnas,** or spiny anteaters, are the only two types of mammals that lay eggs. Zoologists classify platypuses and echidnas together in their own order, or group, called the **monotremes**.

PLATYPUS
FOSSIL

The oldest mammal fossil ever found, an extinct species of platypus, is 110 million years old.

Below, dragonfly naiads are included in the platypus diet
Right, a platypus can swim in icy water

PLATYPUS HABITATS

Wild platypuses live only in eastern Australia and on the island of Tasmania. Though platypuses thrive in captivity, they do not breed when taken out of their natural **habitat.** This is one reason that no zoos outside of Australia keep platypuses.

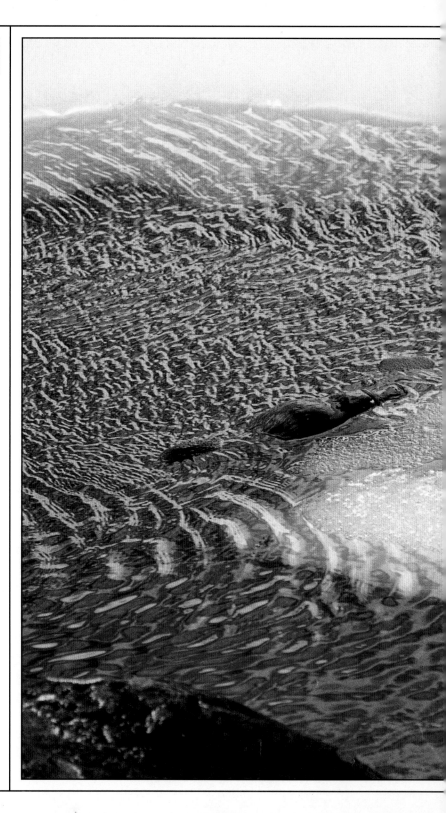

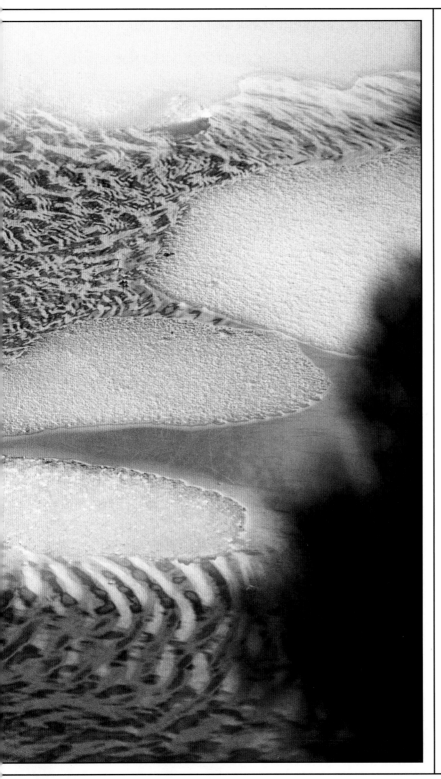

In the wild, the soft earth along river-banks and around lakeshores is perfect for platypus **burrows.** The burrows can range from 15 to 60 feet (4.6–18 m) in length and usually contain many tunnels.

Platypuses are **semiaquatic,** so they need to spend most of their time in water. Webbed feet and a fur-covered paddle tail make the platypus a good swimmer as it hunts for food underwater.

11

PLATYPUS
VOICE

Adult platypuses almost never make a sound; the exception is the low growl they make when they feel threatened.

PLATYPUS
SUCCESS

Only one zoo, located in Healesville, Aus-tralia, has succeeded in breeding platypus-es in captivity.

TRUE OR FALSE?

Platypuses were part of the Ringling Brothers and Barnum & Bailey Circus.

TRUE!

"The Greatest Show on Earth" displayed them in a sideshow.

12

Because it finds food at the bottom of lakes and rivers, the platypus is called a **bottom feeder.** Underwater, the platypus shuts the flap of skin that covers its eyes and ears. **Electrosensors** on the bill help the platypus to locate food. Insect larvae make up most of the platypus' diet; however, crayfish, small snails, and worms make healthy meals as well. Platypuses eat a great deal of food, usually half their own body weight every day.

The platypus needs to surface to breathe

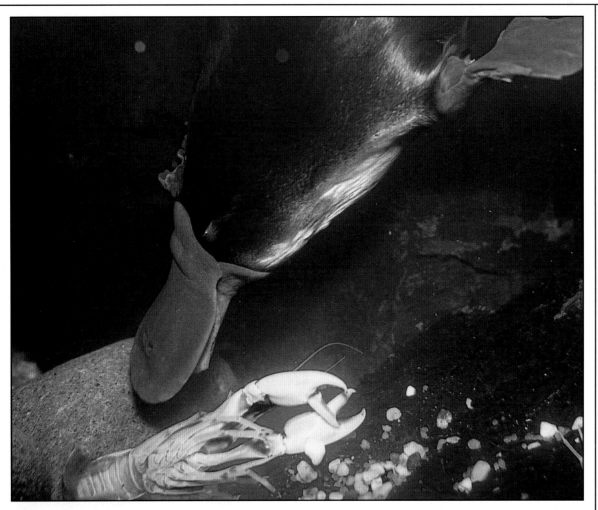

PLATYPUS
BRAIN

Studies show that a large part of the platypus brain is used to understand the messages sent to it by the nerves in its bill.

13

Left, platypuses catch food in the water Above, a dingo

Food and **grit** is gathered underwater, then carried to the surface in the large pouches located inside the animal's cheeks. Using the horny plates in its bill and mouth, the platypus grinds up its catch.

In the summer, platypuses store fat in their tails for the winter ahead, when they have to **forage** for longer periods of time. When in its water environment, the platypus is often safe from predators. However, when on land, the platypus may find itself at the bottom of the **food chain.** This means that it can be an easy meal for larger animals such as hawks, big snakes, foxes, and **dingoes.**

PLATYPUS
FUR

The platypus has the most dense fur of all mammals; only the sea otter comes close to having fur equally dense.

Above, otters have thick fur like platypuses Right, the platypus is built for swimming

PLATYPUS BODIES

Adult platypuses usually measure under 20 inches (50 cm) long and weigh two to three pounds (1–1.5 kg). Platypuses have a sleek shape that helps them speed through water. Two layers of brown or yellowish fur keeps the platypus warm in the water and protects its skin. Short, thick underfur grows close to the skin, trapping air to hold in the animal's body warmth. Long, flat, shiny guard hairs protect the underfur.

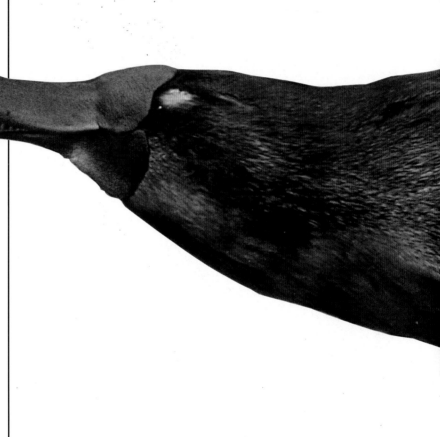

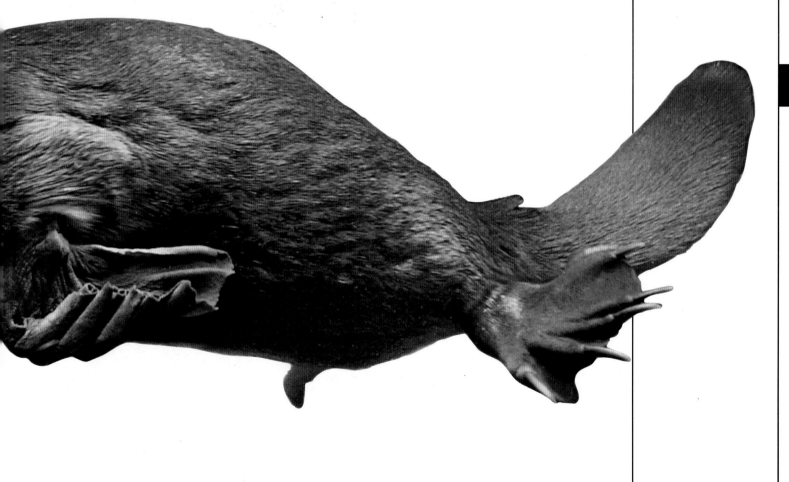

PLATYPUS

Baby platypuses are born with an "egg tooth" similar to that of birds. The tooth, used by the platypus to break out of its egg, soon falls out.

PLATYPUS
PLATES

The horny plates that platypuses have in place of teeth grow constantly; these plates wear down because platypuses eat such gritty food.

Above, snail
Right, the top side of a platypus bill

Despite its name, the duck-billed platypus' bill feels nothing like that of a duck. Bird bills are hard, but the platypus bill is soft to the touch; leathery skin covers the bone and **cartilage.** Tiny holes, each housing an extremely sensitive nerve ending, appear all over a platypus' bill. These electrosensors let the platypus locate its food by *feeling* movements made in the environment.

Platypuses have short legs, and their wide, webbed feet have no fur.

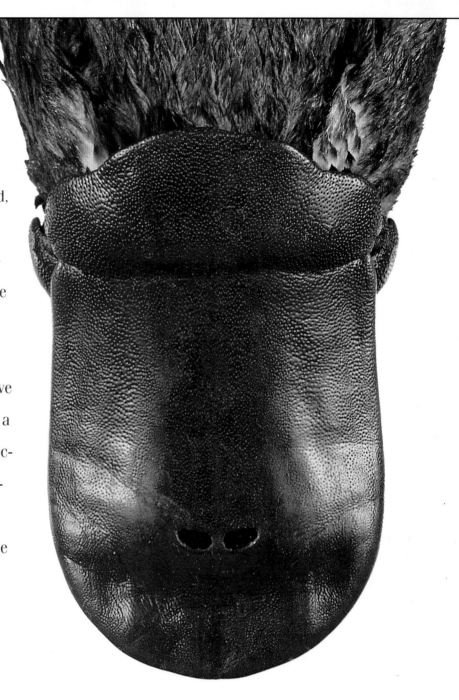

The webbed skin of the front feet stretches far beyond the claws, creating a paddle shape. When swimming, platypuses use the front feet to paddle smoothly through the water. The back feet and broad, flat tail help them to steer. On land, platypuses fold back the webbed skin on their front feet to walk and dig.

17

Above, Australian snake
Left, the bottom side of a platypus bill

PLATYPUS

F A C T

The platypus has a life expectancy of 10 years in the wild.

PLATYPUS

E G G S

A platypus egg is 10 times smaller than a chicken egg. It is softer too—you can squeeze it without breaking it.

Top, goanna
Bottom, wedge-tailed eagle
Opposite, the platypus is very buoyant

Adult male platypuses have long, sharp, hollow spurs on the inside of their hind ankles. These spurs contain **venom.** Used as a weapon in fighting rival platypuses during mating season or in defense against predators, these spurs can be dangerous. They can kill small animals and inflict painful wounds on larger ones. Platypuses are the only mammal species that have venom.

18

PLATYPUS
PLUNGE

The platypus heart-beat falls from an average of 140 beats per minute to 20 beats per minute underwater; this slowing down helps the platypus dive for long periods of time.

*Above, freshwater crocodiles eat platypuses
Right, platypus habitat*

Mating season for platypuses extends from July to October. This is Australia's late winter and early spring. Platypuses go through a **courtship** period. The pair meets in the water, where the male grasps the female's tail.

Together they swim slowly in circles before mating. Little else is known about platypus breeding, as they seldom breed in captivity.

To get ready to lay her eggs, the female platypus digs a nesting burrow. First, she makes an entrance above the water. Then she digs a tunnel as long as 60 feet (18 m), much longer than the burrow she lives in the rest of the year. At the very end she makes a special chamber for her nest. She lines this room with grass and leaves.

Like most mammals, the platypus prefers to be away from others of her species when nesting.

PLATYPUS
F A C T

Compared to other mammals, platypuses have an abnormally low body temperature of 89.6 degrees Fahrenheit (32° C).

21

Platypuses bills are soft and sensitive

Scientists believe that during the earth's Cretaceous period, millions of years ago, the continents drifted apart, separating Australia from Antarctica.

Platypus emerging from its burrow

Finally, the female turns around and plugs the entrance of the tunnel, as well as several other places along the way, with dirt. In the nesting chamber, the female platypus can lay from one to three eggs, though two is most common. The mother must **incubate** her eggs for 8 to 10 days.

PLATYPUS
ANCHORS

Platypuses use the sharp claws on their back feet to anchor themselves to the ground when they're digging with their front feet.

PLATYPUS
FLOAT

Because of the air trapped in the platypus' underfur, these animals are buoyant, which means they easily float on the water's surface.

A platypus can sift food from flowing water

Platypus eggs are one-half inch (1 cm) in length. The shells are not brittle like chicken eggs, but rather they are leathery like those of snakes and lizards. The mother often wraps herself around her eggs while they are incubating. Sometimes she rolls onto her back and holds them on her belly.

PLATYPUS

BROOM

Platypuses use their tails to carry and push dirt out of their way when they dig their burrows.

PLATYPUS

PREDATOR

Goannas are large lizards with powerful bodies and sharp claws; they eat small animals—including platypuses!

Right, platypus using a log to stay under water

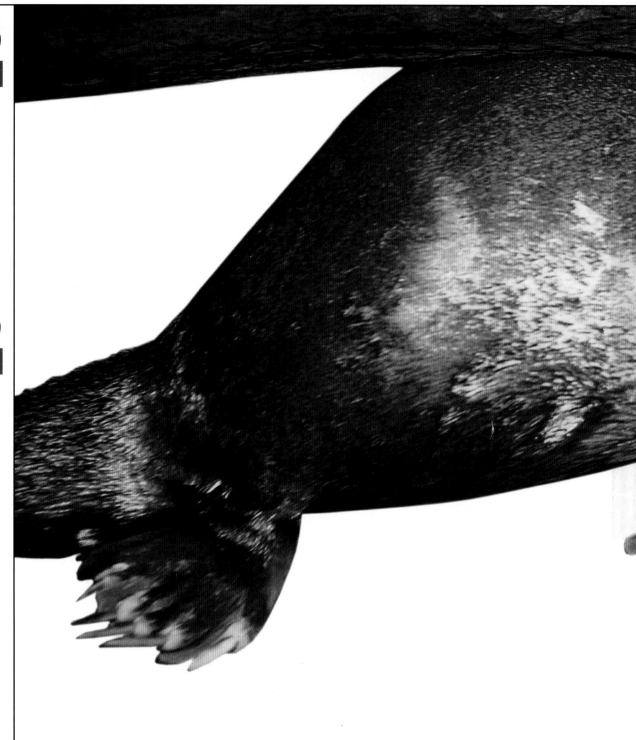

25

PLATYPUS YOUNG

Baby platypuses are born blind and naked. They measure about one inch (2.5 cm) in length. Unlike all other mammals except echidnas, platypuses have no nipples. The mother's milk oozes out of pores on her belly. Scientists used to think the babies simply licked up the milk, but research has now proven they can suckle, even with a bill.

A baby platypus grows fast. The mother first leads her young out of the nesting burrow when it has reached about sixteen weeks of age. Then the mother teaches it how to swim and hunt for food. Platypus young leave the nesting burrows for good when they are five months old. Their bodies are covered with thick fur, and they no longer need their mother's milk. At this age, they've grown to more than one foot (30 cm) in length and are skilled hunters.

Above, platypus digging

PLATYPUS
PLUNGE

Due to their super-thick underfur, platypuses can swim even on days when the temperature falls almost to the freezing point.

PLATYPUS
RECORD

The platypus spends 16 to 18 hours a day in the water, but they have been known to stay in the water up to 26 hours at a time.

Platypuses are very strong divers

BEHAVIOR

Once grown, platypuses leave their mothers and make their own burrows. The platypus is a solitary animal, usually living alone, although for part of the year some platypuses share their burrow with a mate. While several platypus burrows might be located along the same stretch of riverbank or lakeshore, the animals never gather in a large group, as some birds and other mammals often do.

PLATYPUS
S P U R

A platypus spur is made out of keratin, the same substance that makes up human fingernails.

Above, a platypus surfacing
Below, the Tazmanian devil is a nocturnal hunter

Platypuses tend to live in the same place all of their lives; however, a drought may cause a platypus to move. They are **nocturnal** animals and spend almost no time on land except to dig burrows. This is why humans seldom see platypuses in the wild.

Platypuses spend a great deal of time in the stream or lake along which they live. In the water, they dive again and again, searching for food for hours at a time. Usually they spend just a minute or two underwater. To stay submerged longer—up to 11 minutes—the platypus must hold onto something such as a root or log to keep from floating to the surface.

PLATYPUSES AND HUMANS

For thousands of years the Australian **Aborigine** peoples have hunted the platypus to eat. In the past, settlers to Australia also hunted the platypus, but not to eat. Its sleek fur was valuable, and many platypuses were killed. Although platypuses are now abundant in their native lands, urban development threatens platypus habitats. As cities spread out and streams and lakes become polluted, platypuses may suffer.

PLATYPUS POISON

Platypuses have killed dogs using their venom. When a handler was once spurred in the hand, his arm swelled up enormously, and he couldn't use his hand for months.

Left, Cephissus Creek, Tasmania, is a clean platypus habitat

PLATYPUS
FACT

*Young female platy-
puses grow spurs,
which they lose
before adulthood.
Males' spurs don't
contain venom until
they become adults.*

*Above, the venomous
spur of a male platypus
Right, the platypus is an
amazing creature*

In recent years, how-ever, the Australian government has worked hard to protect the platypus. Crab pots and fish traps, once a danger to platypuses that became caught and drowned, are now banned from use. Sanctuaries such as the one in Healesville, Australia, are also helping the platypus to thrive. By sharing platypus infor-mation and studying these animals both in captivity and in the wild, Healesville teaches peo-ple about the important role of this amazing creature in our global ecosystem.

PLATYPUS
FOSSIL

Scientists who found a platypus fossil that is 20 million years old believe that today's platypuses descended from ancient **reptiles.**

PLATYPUS
PROBLEMS

The Australian Gold Rush began in 1851. Many miners traveled to Australia in search of riches and disturbed platypus habitats along riverbanks.

Glossary

An **Aborigine** is one of the native people of Australia or one of their descendents.

A **bottom feeder** is an animal that finds its foods on the bottom of a creek, river, lake, or the ocean.

Burrows are the holes or series of tunnels that small animals dig to live or hide in.

Cartilage is a tissue that's both tough and bendable. Human ears are made of cartilage.

Some animals go through a period of **courtship** before mating; they may make special sounds or perform gestures to "show off" to their mate.

Dingoes are a species of wild dog that live in Australia.

Echidnas, also called spiny anteaters, are close relatives of platypuses; they are monotremes.

Some animals have **electrosensors** that send messages from special nerve endings on the body to the brain; these feelings help the animal find food or avoid danger.

The **food chain** is an order in nature in which plants or tiny animals are eaten by some animals, and those animals are in turn eaten by other, often larger, animals.

To **forage** is to search for food.

Tiny bits of sand or stone is called **grit;** many toothless animals eat grit to help them grind up their food.

A **habitat** is the place where an animal or plant naturally lives and grows.

A **hoax** is a fake, or something that is not true.

When animals **incubate** their eggs, they keep them warm so the eggs will hatch; usually this is done by gently sitting on them or holding them.

A **mammal** is an animal that feeds its young with milk from the mother's body and whose skin is covered with hair or fur.

Monotremes are mammals with characteristics of a reptile; they lay eggs and have reptile-like bone and intestine structure.

Nocturnal animals are more active at night than during the day.

Reptiles are animals that crawl on their bellies (snakes) or on small short legs (lizards) and whose bodies are covered with scales or bony plates.

Animals that are **semiaquatic** live in or near water and spend most of their time in the water; they often feed on plants or animals in the water as well.

Venom is poison created inside the body of certain animals; it if often used as a form of defense.

Index